FALLING DOWN FUNNY

Living With Epilepsy: A View Fro

By MARK HAWKINS

To Sam. You are and will always be the light at the end of my tunnel.

TABLE OF CONTENTS

Chapter 1 – I Have No Idea What Happens When It Happens

I just got off work. I am sitting in my room watching a movie on my computer. I can feel it coming on.

At first I am not even sure it is a seizure. I just know something is wrong. I don't feel right.

It is weird that, after all these years, I don't know the feeling right away. But I don't. Maybe it's because I don't always remember seizures. Maybe it's because the feeling is so faint. Maybe it's because I am already confused and I just don't know it. Whatever. When they don't come pounding on, I always question what is going on.

This one is no different. I spend a minute or two wondering what is wrong with me. I get a little nervous. I always feel like something is...I don't know. Is wrong the right word? I look around for something to explain it. And then it hits me. Shit. Shit. SHIT! It's a seizure. It hasn't started, I still feel OK, but I know now that it's coming. At least I am alone. No one will see it. OK, OK. I can do this. I can get into bed. I can get comfortable. Maybe it won't even happen.

I make a move for the bathroom. I always like to pee beforehand, just in case. That way I lower the chances of soaking my clothes in urine. I have no idea if this has any effect or not, but I like to try. Unfortunately I don't make it. I get to the door of the bathroom and realize I don't have that much time. I will never be able to stand there for the two or three minutes that is going to take. It's coming on too fast now and I should get to the bed. Go! Get to the bed! The last thing I want to do is to fall down in the bathroom with my pants around my ankles. I mean, c'mon. It's bad enough as it is. No need to add a lump on the head.

I take a couple of steps and just fall onto the bed. I grab a pillow and hug it. I really grab the pillow and try to squeeze the feeling away. I am already terribly uncomfortable. It is coming on, but too slowly. My mind is all over the place. I am scared of what's coming. I don't want to have a seizure. Jesus, I don't want this. What could I have done to cause this? It almost...hurts.

I hear something. Shit. It's me. I am groaning. How stupid is that? Why did I do that?

I try to look at the clock to know how long it will last. My mind is not cooperating. I look at my computer, at the movie. It's a war movie and a plane just flew by. I think it was something about a plane, but the images are starting to get rapid and disjointed. I think of flying. I think of the feeling of the plane when it first takes off. I think of swimming. I think of my kids. I think of being a kid. I think of someone I knew when I was a kid. Just...pictures. I remember that I wanted to look at the clock. I am having a hard time focusing.

I just groaned again...I know that...I remember hearing myself...Like I was trying to call out to someone...Trying to call out...DAMMIT! Just do it or end it...I hate this.

It's very close now...close...and it comes...I just go...wherever I go...I have no idea what happens when it happens – I am just gone. Thankfully. Because I know it only gets worse.

I have a hard time getting out of this one. It's not the first time. I remember one time when my wife was with me – and I could hear her calling to me. It was like I was at the bottom of a well. "Mark! Mark!" I wanted to call out to her, but I couldn't. Shit, that was horrible. This one isn't that bad, but similar. I come to the realization that it's pretty much over – but I can't get out. I'm stuck. And I panic. Fuck – it's just about the worst feeling ever. For a couple seconds I am convinced I am going to die right there, in the blackness. Just be there...leave my wife and kids...oh my God...it can't end like this...

And then it's pretty much over. I am lying there, wondering how long it has been going on. I know it's been a while. I am sore. The movie on the computer is over. Shit. I hate this.

I roll over and realize I have peed myself. Again. Man – that's just wrong. At least no one saw it. I can change clothes. Not so bad, I guess.

I am so tired. I close my eyes. I sleep for over an hour in my piss. Who cares? Dried or wet, it's still just my urine.

I get up and take my clothes off. I throw them on the floor. I will deal with them tomorrow. For now I just want to go back to sleep. I turn the computer off. I turn the lights off. I go to the bathroom. You would think there would be less pee, considering how much there seems to be on the bed. But there is quite a bit in there. Interesting.

I walk back to the bed and fall on it. I think I am awake for two or three minutes. I sleep hard. For eight or nine hours. And I wake up feeling like I didn't get enough sleep.

But at least it is over. Until the next time.

Chapter 2 My Life As I Knew It Was Over

My name is Mark Hawkins. I am 43 years old. I am a professional standup comedian. And I have seizures. That certainly doesn't make me special or unique. According to the Center for Disease Control, 2.2 million Americans have epilepsy. Ford Motor Company sold 2.2 million cars last year. There are 2.2 million farms in the United States. Wal-Mart employs 2.2 million people. And there are 2.2 million people like me, falling down all over America.

Because of the seizures, I have been doing comedy almost exclusively on cruise ships for about fifteen years. But more on that later.

For me it began in Lakeland, Florida. Oh, it didn't really start there. I don't know where or when they started. I had been having seizures for a while but I didn't understand I was having them. Lakeland is just the place I can point to as the place where somebody pointed to what was going on and said, "That's a seizure."

Most people are baffled when I say that. "How can you have a seizure and not know it?"

Like most people who travel for work, I lived most of my life alone and the seizures themselves were unlike anything else I had encountered in my life. What made them more difficult to grasp was that I had (and have) no memory of most of the actual events. When the really strong ones (the Grand Mal) hit, I have nothing. I have no memory of any of it. One minute I am standing there and the next minute I wake up on the floor thinking, "That was weird."

So I thought I was having some sort of panic attack. Which was bad. Maybe bad is the wrong word. They were earthshattering. Each event was, at the time, the worst thing that had ever happened to me. All I knew was that something horrible had happened and I never wanted it to happen again. But I didn't think I needed to go to the hospital.

In retrospect I think I was also a little afraid of getting help. I didn't really want to know that anything serious might be wrong. I was moving from town to town so making an "appointment" to see a specialist seemed out of the question. I didn't have any money so I was afraid to find out that I needed any kind of regular help. And once the episode was over I felt OK so it was easy to tell myself, for a while, anyway, that it would go away "on its own." Denial can be very powerful when backed up by poverty and fear.

I was more or less living in hotels and motels at the time, working as a road comedian. That's the term my friends and I used to describe what we did. A "road comedian" was a comedian who lived out of his car, traveling from town to town, from comedy club to comedy club, from show to show, spending maybe eight to ten months a year "on the road." I understand that whole concept is pretty much gone today, but once upon a time it was pretty common for a comic to just "go on the road" and stay there.

I was not a highpriced comedian. I was a guy staying at the Motel 6 or the Super Eight. I was eating peanut butter and jelly and Raman Noodles that I kept in the trunk of my car. An occasional Taco Bell, usually bought from the change found in the car seat cushions, was the highlight of my week. I was living hand to mouth on the $200 to $500 a week I was getting paid from comedy clubs, paying all my own expenses: food, gas, the works. I spent a lot of nights sleeping in my car, dreaming of being able to afford restaurant food or not sleeping in my car when I wasn't working. It was a surprisingly wonderful time, as long as you ignored the whole seizure thing.

I remember sitting in a chair in some dump of a hotel. It was one of those twenty dollars-a-night places where the TV remote control is attached to the bedside table. I was sitting there, watching "Free HBO" and the next thing I knew I was laying on the bed, covered in sweat, my heart pounding. I had pissed myself and I was petrified. I have been asked about this story several times by friends, comics. And just about everyone I tell the story to responds, "There has to be more to this story! It was your first one! You have to have more!"

But there is no more. That, literally, is the whole thing. I don't remember anything else. I only remember watching TV – and then waking up, covered in sweat and urine, and scared. I thought it must have been a panic attack of some sort. I really had no idea what that even meant. And I certainly had no idea what to do about it. But the last thing I was going to do was to call anyone and tell them that I had just "had a panic attack so bad that I pissed myself." I cleaned myself up and hoped it would never happen again.

I wanted to call someone. I was just too embarrassed. I like to think, if I wasn't working on the road, living in hotels at the time, I might have sought some kind of help. I knew this was not something normal. I was not a bedwetter and something obviously was going on. I knew there was something seriously wrong with me. But I was always in another strange town, in another strange motel, surrounded by total strangers, and I really didn't know whom to call. So I bundled up the wet sheets, left them in the corner or my motel room, and moved on with my life. I told myself that whatever had happened would simply never happen again. I wouldn't let it.

I was wrong, of course. It did happen again. And then it started happening regularly.

I was just outside of Erie, Pennsylvania. The gig was a crappy one nighter. That means there was one night's work and not much money. You do this sort of thing a lot when you are a young comedian. The gig was weird because you played both the restaurant and the bar, and they were separated by a little wall. The stage went into both rooms. If you played the restaurant, you had your back to the bar. If you played the bar, you had your back to the restaurant. The only way to be seen by the people in both rooms was to face the blank wall right in front of you and kind of glance to your right and glance to your left into both. It was awkward and difficult. But, hey, it was work. By that I mean you humiliated yourself but you got paid. Which really is the definition of being a young comedian.

The show was late and I had a few beers afterwards. I was very tired. I got up early and drank a Mountain Dew. I got behind the wheel and hit the road, working my way through a huge coffee.

I don't remember much of what happened next. I was still in complete denial about what had happened the first time. I don't think I was even allowing myself to think about it. I certainly was not aware of the sensations surrounding a seizure. It was all very confusing to me. But everything got faster and faster. I threw my coffee out the car window. I had just consumed too much caffeine. That was it, I thought. I was having some sort of caffeine overdose. I was rolling down the Interstate so I just kept driving. But the feeling got worse. At one point I started to think I was having a heart attack so I pulled the car over. It continued to get worse. The next thing I remember, I was laying next to my car, in a ditch along the side of the road, with my heart pounding. My car was still running, other cars were flying by at 75 miles an hour, and I was just lying there; sweating, confused, heart pounding.

It was easy to just put the supposed panic attacks out of my mind when they were not happening. "That could have been anything," I told myself. It was stress. Alcohol. Caffeine. Sleepdeprivation. Who knows? I tried not to think about it. Then it would happen again. It quickly became harder to explain, even to myself. It quickly moved from "something that happened" to "something that I do."

I had wracked my brain for answers and there were none. I wrote pages in my notebook and tried to work out the problem myself. Of course, the answers never came. I am not a doctor. I was just a guy who freaked out and pissed himself. My life seemed to be quickly spinning out of control.

I tried Tai Chi. I started meditation. I started smoking a lot of pot. I was sure that the answer was in learning how to relax.

I loved being a comic, and I didn't want that life to end. Something told me that any sort of call for help would drag me home. The last thing I wanted was to end up back at my parents' house.

The road is a wonderful place for a young, single, albeit poor comedian. There are women. There is free alcohol and pot. There is no end to the parties. Despite the fact that you are often treated poorly and it is a pretty hard life, I cannot think of a better way to make a living.

But then came March of 1993 and Lakeland, Florida. One of the great things about being on the road is that you can pretty much make your own schedule. I used to make several trips a year to Walt Disney World in Orlando, and St. Patrick's Day used to be one of my favorite times to go. It is not what it used to be there, but in 1993 it was a great party. Pleasure Island, until recently, was the "bar district" at Disney World. They had green beer, they had Irish Bands, and they had midgets dressed up as leprechauns, running around Pleasure Island passing out "gold." It was very funny, even considering how offensive some people thought it was.

Some friends and I went to Disney for St. Patrick's Day, and then I went back to Lakeland to stay with my friend Danny to avoid paying for a hotel room. A poor comic like me would do anything to avoid paying for anything when he could.

Danny is probably my oldest friend. His father and my father are best friends so we grew up together. As sports writers, both of our fathers got to escape Michigan's often brutal winters each February, and spend the next two months in Lakeland, Florida where the Detroit Tigers baseball team held their Spring Training. Those are some of my fondest memories. It never mattered that the hotel was terrible and there wasn't all that much to do. We were children in an amazing new place. It was wonderful.

Danny had grown up to also work for the Detroit Tigers and he now had a room at that same shitty hotel where we had spent so many springs together, so the hour drive was well worth the effort. We met up for an amazing trip to St. Patrick's Day at Disney World (which Danny also has a fondness for) and spent the night in his free hotel. It was a great night.

I woke up the next day at his place. I remember the feeling coming and I tried to take myself to the bathroom. I have no idea why I was going to the bathroom. In retrospect, it was probably just one of those seizure things: Your mind does things that don't make logical sense afterwards. In my addled mind, something told me to go there. Maybe I just didn't want Danny to see me have the attack. Who knows?

I remember turning on the shower. Maybe I was trying to cover the sound of whatever happened. Maybe I thought Danny would think I had decided to take a shower. Maybe I thought I would need to clean my clothes when I woke up. While I was still pretty new to the world of seizures for me, they didn't even have a name yet I had had five or six episodes at this point. I was familiar enough with the events that would follow.

I woke up outside the bathroom and Danny was looking at me and he was a hell of a lot more upset than I was.

From my perspective, I had gone to the bathroom, turned on the water and then woke up on the floor. To Danny, of course, there was more to the story. I have no idea what "the rest of the story" is – and to this day, we have never spoken of what happened in between.

Danny called the Detroit Tigers' team doctor. At least I think he called the doctor. I actually have no idea who he called. He called someone and someone called back on the phone. I didn't like the idea. Like I said, my father is a sports writer from Detroit and I grew up around the team so the man knew who I was and knew my father. I talked to him briefly and he told me to go to the local hospital for a couple of tests. I didn't want to go, but better to see a doctor in Lakeland, Florida, than have my family find out about my problems. So I went.

I wasn't expecting anything. As I said, I thought these were panic attacks. I really thought I was going to be in there for fifteen minutes and some doctor would tell me to "relax." I thought he was going to act like I was being an idiot. "Drink less. Cut down on caffeine. Get more sleep." The usual admonitions. I really wasn't expecting...well, anything. So I was pretty flippant about the whole thing.

I certainly was completely unprepared when the doctor came in and told me that I had tested positive for grand mal seizures. He asked me if I had ever had anything like this before. I said yes. More than one? Yes. Just this week? No, I think for about a year.

"You need to go home and see a neurologist," the doctor said. I began to realize that this was probably not a simple thing after all. The doctor told me all the other things I needed to do: Get more sleep. Make sure I stayed hydrated. Don't drink too much. No drugs. Eat right.

And driving is out of the question.

I was shocked. I was horrified. I truly believed life as I knew it was over. I mean, how can I be a working comedian with no car? I thought about this for the next two days as, contrary to doctor's orders and, in retrospect, contrary to common sense I drove the twenty hours from Florida to my parent's house.

As I drove home, I thought about all the crap I had recently gone through. Those panic attacks had been, in fact, a series of blackouts. I had been flopping around the floor and doing whoknowswhat. There was a piece of my life that I was missing. There was part of my life that was completely out of control. There was, in fact, another person inside of me that came out and took over every once in a while. I felt like a werewolf, a vampire, a zombie. I am a completely normal person strolling along the shore until the full moon rises, at which time the monster comes out. There is some "Mr. Hyde" whom I don't know but everyone else sees.

I was told that I was not supposed to drink anymore. That was not such a big loss. I gave it up a week later and didn't drink again for years. But I got good and drunk on principle the night before I had to give it up.

I had to go home, and the woman I was dating at the time was pretty upset that I wouldn't "swing out" the fifteen hours to Little Rock, Arkansas, to see her on my way home. She could not fathom what was going on. She did not like the idea that I was willing to drive my car to my parent's house but not willing to drive to her house on the way. She didn't understand how I could suddenly "become" a seizure patient. I didn't sound or seem sick. To this day, I think she believed I was making it all up. In all of her letters and phone calls to me, she never mentioned it once.

Our relationship sputtered along for a couple more weeks, only because I was too lazy to put it out of its misery on that first phone call. I just kind of watched it limp around and bleed for a while. But, sure enough, it died eventually.

I was also told that, like all seizure patients, I could not drive anymore. Of course, I made my living on the road as a comedian. That meant plenty of driving. I instantly lost my job with the news. I thought about that long and hard while I drove my car the twenty hours back to Detroit.

What can I say? This is not the story of a good patient.

Chapter 3 - Flying Under the Radar

I have just finished working a five-day cruise. I got off the ship in Galveston, Texas, an hour ago and now I'm sitting in the backseat of a van heading to the Houston airport to get on a plane to fly home. My flight is in a couple hours.

I am pleased to report that I didn't drink last night. I got a good night's sleep and I ate a good breakfast this morning. I can't think of any reason why I should feel weird. But I do. Something isn't right.

I have that terrible feeling that I know what's going on but I can't for the life of me think of what it is. I hope I am wrong. Wait – that doesn't make any sense. I have a little bit of a stomach ache.

It starts to feel more like something else. Something familiar. Something horrible. Something that sets my nerves on edge. I try to get comfortable, but that isn't happening.

I lean back in the van's seat. I lean against the window. I try to sprawl back with my legs extended. But nothing helps.

All at once, I know what's going on. I am having a seizure. I can hear myself saying, "Fuck, fuck, fuck." Then I look around, embarrassed, to see if anyone actually heard me. I don't know if I am more embarrassed because I just said, "Fuck" or worried that I am about to have a seizure. Because they scare the shit out of me.

I consider telling the guy sitting next to me that I am epileptic. I could say something like, "Don't worry if I flop around and piss myself." That would get his attention. I don't know why what other people think of me when I have a seizure makes me so embarrassed. But everyone acts so horribly when they find out I am epileptic.

I decide saying something is not worth it. I decide to take my chances on the fact that this might be a small one.

I start moving from position to position in my seat, quite quickly, trying to relax. Nothing is helping. I am getting more and more uncomfortable.

I catch myself groaning out loud at one point and look at the person next to me again to see if he is staring at me. But he is listening to his Ipod. Thank God. I think it would have been worse if he were watching.

I check the clock. It feels close now. I like to know how long they last. It is 8:00 a.m. 8:00 a.m. exactly. That's weird. I wonder if that has anything to do with it? I wonder if there is some weird power when it is exactly on the hour? Things are starting to make no sense.

It is getting bad. It's almost here. I try to lay down in my seat with my feet on the front seat of the van. In any normal setting this would be horribly rude. Fuck it. Let them be mad.

I am freaking out now. Panic is setting in. I can feel the sweat. I am afraid of how bad it is going to be. I am trying to fight it off. I wish it would just come and be over with.

What's going on? Am I drunk? Did someone drug me?

The sun comes in the van window and I realize how hot I am. I visualize the sun. I think of the months I spent living in the California Desert with my sister, when she was sick. I think of being a child again. I think of childhood friends. I think of a friend I knew in college. I think of the smell of the food in my college dorm. A smell in the van wakes me up.

I slowly straighten up and look at the clock. It is 8:16 a.m.

I am in a deep state of panic. Each of these thoughts has some element that scares me in some way, though when I look back on them, I cannot for the life of me remember why.

My head is still swimming. I look around the van to see if I have done anything to call attention to myself. Is anyone staring? Has it been bad? Everyone is still doing his or her own thing. The guy next to me is still engrossed in his Ipod. He has no idea what has happened on the seat next to him. Thank God. Or maybe he is just pretending not to see.

It is starting again.

Shit. Shit. Shit. It's bad. It's much worse than the first one.

I keep telling myself I am not dying. I am going to be OK. It's just a seizure. But I am not sure. There is a moment, there is always a moment, where I am sure I am about to die.

I stop fighting it and let it happen. I close my eyes and go.

I wake up when the van stops at Houston's Hobby Airport. I do not get off here. This is not my airport. I have to stay on the van until we get to Bush Airport, about another half an hour away. I am tired and sore, like I've just gone through a strenuous workout. It is 9:27 a.m. Fuck. I have had another seizure and fallen asleep. Maybe the seizure lasted over an hour. I can't believe that though. That doesn't seem right.

I sit up. My neck hurts. At least my pants are dry. I didn't piss myself this time. I look for something to drink. I don't have anything. Man, I am really thirsty.

I don't look at anyone for the rest of the trip. I don't know these people and I don't want to know them. They are now diseased to me now – people who are "tainted." In my mind, they carry with them the memory of this experience. Maybe if I don't look, I will forget who they are.

When we finally arrive at the airport, I get off the van quickly. I don't look at anyone. I don't tip the driver. I walk as quickly as I can through the doors and join the masses of people in the airport. The quicker I can become one of them, the quicker I will become invisible. Once I blend in, I will no longer be "the guy who just had a seizure in the van." I will just be another anonymous individual rushing to catch a plane.

By the time I pass through security and get something to eat, I start to believe I am just like everyone else again. I melt into the crowd. No one knows me or anything about me. I'm just another lonely guy who looks like crap at the airport.

Chapter 4 - "At Least I'm Not THAT Guy."

My parents were very nice about my new situation, though, in retrospect, they have never really gotten comfortable with it. My father still doesn't like to talk about it. I am not sure why. I'll admit that for years I didn't like to talk about it either, but I was the one banging his head on the table on the way down. It was a hard adjustment for me but I have finally made my peace with it. I am not sure why he hasn't. But I have kids of my own now, so I guess there is a part of me that can look at my kids and realize it would be a lot harder for me to deal with their problems than my own.

The first thing I had to do when I got home was find a neurologist. I quickly came to realize I am not a big fan of going to the neurologist. I really hate going to the neurologist.

Go to a neurologist's waiting room. There are people drooling; there are people wearing hockey helmets. There are people with obvious severe mental problems. In fact, the only people in the room without some sort of obvious major issue are the sad and tired looking caregivers who trade silently sympathetic and knowing looks when one of the patients is having a particularly "bad day". It's one of the reasons I can't stand going to that office: When I am there, I cannot escape the fact that I am one of them.

Yes, these are my people. I can put my denial into high gear when I am outside, when I am with my "normal" friends, when I am smoking pot in my parent's house and trying to pretend I am eighteen again. But when I am sitting there, waiting to see the doctor, there is no escape. This is my life and these are my people. I, too, am someone with a major neurological disorder and my life is probably closer to these people's lives than to those of the guys I hang out with. I have more in common with these people than I do with my "friends" from high school.

OK, so I don't hang out with these people. I don't actually know these people. But I should. We would get along. We would have a lot more to talk about and no one would make horrible jokes about dancing "like an epileptic" or watching a fish flopping around in the bottom of the boat like it was "totally having a seizure."

People who have never seen me have a seizure rarely believe I have them. "You do not," they say incredulously. My favorite comment is: "You don't look epileptic!" What does an epileptic look like? Am I supposed to be shaking all the time?

My friends still tell me to "stop talking like that." They tell me I am being silly. They say that we are friends and those people have very little in common with me. And yet each person who finds out I have seizures still gets weird about it. Most don't even believe me. "No – are you serious?" "You're kidding." "Really?"

Based on some half-remembered lecture from high-school health class, some people like to pretend they know all about it and make a big deal about their wide range of medical knowledge. They walk around looking for an opportunity to stick something in my mouth. Have you ever woken up with someone's wallet stuffed in your mouth? Your life has gotten pretty low when you have a pair of jeans covered in your own piss and someone is standing over you, staring at their leather wallet, complete with condom ring, jammed in your mouth, and they are waiting – just waiting – for you to say, "Thank you."

I always make my neurology appointments early in the morning. I try to be the first one. It's not always easy but I do my best. And I try to get them to let me in early – before the really depressing people show up.

But then I'm a comic. I wear shoes that don't match. I wear colorful hats. I wear weird T-shirts and clothes to draw attention to myself. I'll bet some of the really messed-up patients are looking at me just like I look at them. Those guys are thinking to themselves, "At least I'm not that guy."

But I still can't deal with the really bad cases sitting there in the office, like the old ladies dealing with cancer and the problem kids who scream and fall down. There are always a couple wheelchairs with incurable people who clearly have dozens of seizures every day. Thank God I'm not them. The really depressing stuff is usually in the afternoon, though. My understanding is it takes these guys a while to get going in the morning.

I hate going to the neurologist because it ruins your whole day. You can't get around it. I always try to make friends with my neurologist – it helps. After an hour of listening to how you haven't gotten any better, you feel like you should be wearing a hockey helmet as well.

I hate it because, except for these reminders, I feel completely normal most if the time. It's like having the hiccups. You have them, and then they are gone. Nothing. No side effects, no nothing. It's over. Unfortunately, that's where the similarity between hiccups and seizures ends. It's kind of like comparing a slap in the face to getting run over by a Mack truck: both are going to leave a mark, but it's a matter of degree. Another difference is that with seizures, you cannot escape the fact that you had it. You think about it and think about it, depending upon how many people saw it. If I am alone when I have it, I can usually completely forget about it pretty quickly – as long as there was no blood involved. When you are in public, everyone will stare and talk for days. "So, you're epileptic, huh?" "No," I say, "I just do that for a laugh."

I developed something called osilopsy at one point where my eyes would shake back and forth. It really didn't mean anything, but it always happened in the morning and just added to the fact that I felt like an outcast. I still have no idea what caused it. My neurologist thought it was a side effect of the medication I was on at the time. It went away after about a year so I didn't give it much thought. But it was really annoying at the time. You want to see the freak? Look at the guy with one eye wiggling back and forth. "Shit. At least I'm not that guy. Look at him! He has a jiggly eye!"

The tests at the neurologists are not that bad once you get used to them. But they all were horribly intimidating the first time I saw them. And, of course, I was always alone.

There was the MRI – or as I call it, "the tunnel of horrors." The first time you have an MRI it is painfully intimidating. Once you become good at it it's just a really boring test but the first time is horrific.

You are laid out on an uncomfortable plastic table. Then that table is moved into a tube that barely fits a person. You lay there for an ungodly period of time completely surrounded by loud machinery and you are not allowed to move, while this big magnet moves around and takes a picture of your brain.

It's loud and claustrophobic. It's cold and annoying. And every time you try to scratch your nose or something, there is a voice that is piped into the tube that says, "Please stop moving." It's horrible.

And I'm not kidding about the time. This test can take hours! There you are just lying on a table stuffed into a tube that is only an inch or so above your entire body.

The good places let you bring a CD. I prefer books on tape because, if you listen to music, you have a tendency to move a little. Then you get this voice in your head again. "Please stop moving." Crappy places just put on their own music and for some reason lab technicians listen to really shitty music.

I have no idea what the correlation is between lab techs and shitty music but it's totally true. I mean, you would think lab techs would listen to cool music. These are smart people. These are cool people. These are nice people. I would have anticipated some pretty cool music. Nope! The older the lab techs are, the more they try to please everyone so you are sure to get stuff absolutely no one listens to: Kenny G, Garth Brooks, Celine Dion. The younger lab techs are the more "hip." They try to "introduce you" to bands you have never heard of and would never waste your time listening to. You are sure to get a comment on your way out like, "So, what'd you think of that band? Yeah, that's my boyfriend." Or, "That's my buddy, Steve."

Mostly, you just lay there. You have no idea how long you have been in there and no idea how much time you have left to be in there. Time moves slowly and no one talks to you, except to say "stop moving" every five to ten minutes.

I was very angry the first time I did an MRI. They told me the test showed "nothing." Of course it showed nothing! I don't have seizures! I could have told you that! And so why can't I stop coming here?

I find the EEG much more pleasant, though no less intimidating the first time. Electrodes are glued all over the chest and head and then blinky lights are flashed at you while you sit in the dark for an hour or so.

The first time is bad because you don't know what to expect. You feel like a victim in a sci-fi movie as you wait for a jillion volts to come crashing into your body. The tech sits there, staring at you, and you both sit in silence. Horrible, terrible silence...waiting for whatever it is that is going to happen.

But the moment never comes. That's the test. You just sit there. For like an hour. Once you know that, the test is kind of a joke. Cover you with stickum and watch you in the dark. I can do that.

I should mention that taking that stuff off is a real pain in the neck and no one seems particularly interested in the process. You are usually just handed a tissue and your clothes. The tissue dissolves into the stickum and you end up just putting your clothes on and taking a shower when you get home. It really is disgusting stuff.

Most places have you sit in a big comfy chair. And EEG techs seem to be pretty nice, on the whole. Usually middle-aged moms. A good group.

I always fall asleep during the EEG. No one says, "Stop moving," but they do say, "Wake up" every once in a while. Like I said, I like to make my appointments early in the morning.

But I suppose the real reason I don't like the neurologist's office is the fact that I still have seizures. All that time, all that money, all those drugs, and I might as well be back at square one. It's not their fault. I know that. About a quarter of all seizure patients never get "controlled." But I can't help feeling the way I feel. Emotions are irrational and hard to control. I don't know why I still put myself through it all.

Shit. At least I'm not THAT guy.

Chapter 5 - "I Hope I Don't Look Too Bad."

I have just come off stage. The back lounge on the cruise ship that I am working on is not that big but it was very crowded for the late night show. There were nearly five hundred people packed in there tonight and now I am standing outside the showroom door, thanking members of the audience as they file out, when, suddenly, there it is again: That feeling.

I am unfamiliar with it at first and, sadly, I always am. I should not be, since I have been here so many times before. Yet for some reason I never recognize it at the beginning. It is far away, more like a memory or something I forgot to do. The only thing I can say about it is, it makes me nervous.

I go into auto-pilot, shaking hands and smiling at passing guests, while, inside, I focus on IT. Was there something I was supposed to do? Was there somewhere I was supposed to be? Shit. What is that?

As it gets a little worse, it hits me. I think this is a seizure. Again, I am not sure at this point; it is still too far away and too faint. In the early stages, I have this feeling that I can do something about it. Maybe if I just relax it will go away. Maybe I am just thirsty. Maybe I am just tired. Maybe working myself up is what brings it on in the first place, like some kind of self-induced panic attack. But that is never the case. Whether I focus on it or not, it comes on harder and worse. I know now -- it's a seizure.

I turn and just walk away from the line of people patiently waiting to shake me hand and talk to me. I don't say anything. I just leave. They can think what they want about my performer's ego, "What the hell is wrong with that guy? I wanted to tell him a joke." The last thing I want to do is fall down right there in front of them. I have to go. I have to go fast. I have to make my way somewhere, somewhere no one can see me.

There is a "crew only" elevator about fifty feet down the hallway that I can take down to my cabin. I head there but I only get about halfway down the corridor when I realize I am probably not going to make it. It is coming faster and it's coming pretty strong. I am scared. Things are starting to not make sense. Focus, man. Get to the door. Get in there. Get to the elevator.

I start trying to distract my mind to stave off the seizure for just a little while longer until I can escape to safety. "I think that's Coach Bibbs," I say to myself (Coach Bibbs was a track coach I worked with for about six months in college. I barely knew the man.)

"Maybe I should drink a beer?" "I am going golfing tomorrow – what club do I need to hit from here to my cabin? I could hit a four-iron all the way to the casino from here." "I remember when my wife and I went to Vegas, that was a good time." The mind games almost worked too. Or, I don't know, maybe they didn't do anything.

I make it to the door leading to the crew elevator. Unfortunately, I do not make it all the way into the elevator. Instead, I fall down on the floor.

I can hear people talking about me but I have no idea who they are. "What should we do?" "Call 911." "Does he work here?"

I try to say something, but I can hear my voice and it is not coming out right. At least I am not having a grand mal. I like having grand-mal seizures. You just black out and it's over. During petit-mal seizures you have to stay awake the entire time and experience the misery and any embarrassment that comes with it. I would rather just be out for the whole thing. I hate this.

I can hear a man on the ship's phone telling someone where I am, describing the whole scene. I don't remember now exactly what he said, but I remember thinking "C'mon man, I don't look like that!"

When I kind of come out of it and stand back up, my first thought is that I am still going to have another seizure. I think this was just the "warm up." I press the button for the elevator and the five or six crew members standing there are arguing with me to wait for the nurse, who is on her way. I do not wait. I just get into the elevator, thanking them for being so kind. At least I think I thanked them. Again, the memory is not very clear.

Somebody says, "Go with him." I'm sure I heard that. And although I did not really pay attention to him, I remember noticing a man in the elevator with me on the way down and thinking, "This guy is watching me go to my cabin. That's nice of him. Now go away."

I walked down the narrow hallways toward my cabin and – shit. The Captain, the Staff Captain, and the Hotel Director are all right there in front of me. Everyone I work for on board the ship is standing in the hallway next to the door to my cabin. I try really hard to pull it together and smile.

'Gentlemen, how are you this evening?"

I get warm smiles from everyone. I hope that means I don't look too bad.

I put the key in my door. Thankfully nobody follows me into my cabin. I drop my suit jacket on the floor and fall onto the bed. I lay there for – who knows how long? – and sleep. When I wake up I decide to try and write down what just happened to me.

Shit. I still feel like more is coming. But I have to go back to work on stage in about fifteen minutes. The show must go on. A whole new audience will be waiting. This should be interesting.

Chapter 6 - I Do Not Have "Fits"

Let me say this: I do not have "fits." I hear that word all the time and I hate it. Little babies have fits. "I wanna lolly pop! I wanna lolly pop!" That's a "fit." Oddly enough, shoving your wallet into a kid's mouth in that instance would probably be effective. But I digress. I don't have fits. I have seizures.

By the time I had been to the neurologist's office a half-dozen times, and living at my parent's house for about two months, I started to question my own sanity. I was waking up in places I didn't remember going. I was pissing myself. I was going to the neurologist and hanging out with people who clearly had severe mental disorders. They told me I had one as well. I was taking some pretty heavy medication that had some horrible side effects.

My life was not going as planned.

I tried to tell myself that nothing had changed. Every time I had a doctor's appointment, I told my family and friends almost nothing that transpired. "He gave me a prescription," I would say. That was it. Probably as a result, and probably because I am an idiot, I soon went back out on the road as a comedian, driving from gig to gig. I have no way to explain it and no way to rationalize why I did it. I was stupid and I knew it was wrong. I think I just didn't know what else to do.

I got back in the car and went back on the road. A couple of weeks later I had a seizure in a Super Eight in Aberdeen, South Dakota.

Aberdeen is the national home of Super Eight. Everything is the "Super Eight" in Aberdeen and the Super Eights are pretty nice there. Much nicer than in the rest of the country. Hell, they even have restaurants called "Super Eight" in Aberdeen. They are very proud of their homegrown hotel chain. One does not besmirch the name of Super Eight in South Dakota. It is like driving a Japanese car into an Auto Workers Union bar in Detroit. You just don't do it – you are flipping off the local livelihood. Of course, the power of the auto industry in Detroit isn't what it was when I was a kid.

Anyway, I was taking a Super Eight shower one morning, and the next thing I knew, I was laying on the floor with blood streaming down the drain. It was one of those seizures that came out of nowhere. I had hit my head on a protruding soap dish on my way down. I was lying on an odd angle with my face pressed against the wall. It was uncomfortable and I must have been lying there a while because my neck hurt. I had to do the show that night with a napkin taped to my head with scotch tape. Now that's funny.

They were coming regularly now. To the point where having a seizure was the first thing that I thought about when I walked into any room. I looked at the floor to see if it had a nice, lush carpet. I would look for a couch to see if there was a place to fall down should the need arise. I would search for the best "escape route."

"Hey, nice place. Shag carpet." If I go down, I am going down right there!

It never really made much difference. My little plans never seemed to work out. Each time I had a really nice plan worked out in the event of a seizure, I wouldn't have one. And the times I did have a seizure, it came out of nowhere and I never had a plan.

I remember all of this. Except I don't remember why I didn't just drive home from Lakeland, Florida, after my first "official" seizure, park my car, and find a job that didn't require me to put my life, and the lives of everyone else on the highway, in jeopardy every day. And I did this, mind you, for a couple hundred dollars a week -- minus expenses, of course.

Chapter 7 - A Lifetime of Bad Memories

I'm sitting in my cabin watching an episode of "Hung," which is an HBO series that was filmed in Detroit. The scene shows the outside of a bar across the street from a friend's house and I have a strange memory of walking by it, some twenty years ago. A terribly vivid memory.

There is nothing particularly interesting about the memory. We are just three men walking down the street, heading out at the beginning of an evening of drinking. To be honest, it was a great night. But the memory flashes into my head and it is frightening.

And then it's gone, leaving only the horror. It's like someone just showed me a picture of my death and then took it away – and now I have to remember the picture because someone in there is the clue that can save my life. I try harder and harder to remember the image – but it is hard to get a hold of. Each time I get a piece of it, I get more scared.

The bar. The street. Matt was there. Chris was there. Each piece makes my heart pound harder. I know time is moving faster because the TV show has ended. I think I was only halfway through it. Maybe...maybe ten minutes have gone by.

I realize I am about to have a seizure. That's something. I often don't know I am going to have them and just wake up on the floor. Maybe I can get to the bed – wake up in a decent position. It is still going to suck – but being on the bed helps. A little.

I don't really stand up – they come pretty fast sometimes. I kind of dive on the bed. I push on my stomach to see if I have to pee. I hate when I piss myself. Even alone it just sucks. Bladder seems empty.

I move a pillow. More comfortable.

I close my eyes. It's right there. It's right there. Jesus. I can feel it coming. The fucker. I hate it. Why does this happen? Holy shit. No.

And then it's over.

The pillow is on the floor. I am turned the other way. I am covered in sweat and my body hurts like I just ran a couple miles. And I am tired – always tired.

I am confused. There are always things I have a hard time making out. I check the time to see how long I have been out – but I can't remember what time it was when I dove onto the bed. I set the alarm for an hour before I have to go to work because I know I am going to fall asleep. I am tired. Really tired. And there's piss on the bed – God dammit. I hate that. But I will deal with that later. Too tired. Just sleep on the floor for now.

Chapter 8 - "The Little Girl Is Dead" -- And You Killed Her

I have been asked several times why, exactly, I got back behind the wheel of a car when I knew full well that it was a mistake. The truth is that I don't know why, except that I could not for the life of me think of doing anything else with my life other than comedy. And I could not think of any other way to do comedy except by getting these gigs. And to do these gigs required driving. It was as simple as that.

I have also been told that is a poor excuse. When I say, "Comedy is not what I do, it is who I am," it makes perfect sense to me. But when I read it, it is, indeed, a poor excuse. I should have just given up comedy right then and there and done something else with my life. But I didn't. I'm sorry.

I should also point out that I never really wanted fame or fortune. I have never done comedy competitions or festivals. I have never auditioned for a sit-com or a movie. I just love my job. I love standing in front of a live audience and telling jokes. I write jokes and bits six to eight hours a day and tell new jokes every night. It's what I enjoy doing. I can't fathom doing anything else. So I got in a car to do it. Because that was what I had to do.

I was on the road, driving to a gig on Interstate 40, coming into Oklahoma City.   I was, as they say, in the middle of nowhere. It's a great stretch of road, I-40. Nothing but cows and fences and rolling hills that allow you to see for miles. You can't help but realize you are in the middle of nowhere. Every couple miles there is billboard. Otherwise, nothing. Maybe a truck stop. Maybe a McDonalds. Maybe something else that you have no interest in. You really have to find ways to stay awake. I have no idea how truck drivers do it.

Oklahoma City was a great gig. I loved it. The owner of the club was the bastard son of one of the richest families in town and we got along great. We were about the same age. We talked baseball and watched movies.

I had moved over to his club while I was working for a different club on the other side of town. The owners of that particular establishment got into some sort of tussle and split up. The disgruntled owner moved directly across the street and opened a new club with the intention of putting his ex- partner out of business. The battle got nasty, and when I suddenly found myself caught in the middle of dueling megaphones and confused, disgusted customers, I called the club on the other side of town, explained my situation and offered to work for them.

The owner of that club gave me a week of work a couple months down the road, and it quickly became one of my favorite stops. I worked there four times in the next year.

I was on the highway leading into Oklahoma City, about an hour from the club, rolling along in the middle of nowhere and nothing -- and, suddenly, I was on the shoulder of the road, about to hit a motorcycle.

I swerved and clipped the bike. Not too bad, really. I don't know how I did it, but I managed to avoid a major accident. I just touched him. Minutes later, when we were standing on the side of the road, both shaken, I discovered I had simply bent his muffler a bit.

But it was, understandably, an emotional moment for the man. And for me. He had his little girl on the back of his bike. He was visibly upset and he was screaming at me. I apologized profusely. I didn't know what else to do. I could not take my eyes off his daughter, who was standing there crying. I could have easily killed her and her father.

Another car pulled up. The man's wife, the little girl's mother, had been following behind the motorcycle. The man was on his way to sell the bike. I kept apologizing.

We traded insurance information and we all drove off. But I knew that, as much as I had fought it, I could not continue to drive. I should have gotten off the road right after the seizure in Lakeland, Florida, but I didn't. I kept driving and this was the signal that I truly needed to stop before something horrible happened.

I called my mother back in Michigan and asked her fly to Oklahoma City to drive me home. I cancelled all of my work for the rest of the year. My life as a road comic was over.

The drive home was horrible. My mother drove and I just stared out the window, watching my life drift by. We didn't talk. We just drove. Then things got worse. Much worse.

When I got home, I received a phone call from the insurance company. They told me that I had killed the little girl on the motorcycle. "The little girl is dead," he said. I couldn't believe it. I had stood there talking to her. I hadn't even knocked the man off the bike.

I was in a daze for a couple of days. I didn't know what to think. Killed her? When she and parents drove away from the accident, she didn't have a scratch on her. I hadn't even knocked the guy over. Suddenly, I feared I would be paying for it for the rest of my life. Would I go to jail? And that little girl. Dead? How? I couldn't get her out of my mind.

I don't think my parents knew what to say. They were very quiet about the entire thing. It was Friday when the insurance company called to tell me that the girl had died. The man who called said he would call back on Monday to give me the details. "Details?"

I didn't do anything over the weekend. I couldn't. I tried to act like everything was OK. But, of course, it wasn't. Everything was quickly going terribly wrong. And it was all my fault. I had just killed a little girl. Killed a little girl! Although, my eyes told me I had just bent the muffler on her dad's motorcycle. What exactly did she die of? How could she be dead?

On Monday, the insurance man called me back. All he said was that he had made a mistake. A mistake? He had looked at the wrong file. The little girl was fine. My accident was nothing: a simple bump and I shouldn't worry about it. Couple hundred dollars damage at the most. He would not need to talk to me again.

I was too stunned to be angry. No apology for the hell he had just put me and my family through. No explanation. All he said was, "Your girl is fine." That was it.

I had no idea how to react. I still don't whenever I think about it.

My life was still over. Sure, it was better than it had been the day before. But I was still an unemployed and broke nobody who fell down every once in a while and pissed himself on occasion. Except for the fact that I was no longer about to be put on trial for manslaughter, my situation hadn't changed.

I was back to living at my parents house again. Going to see the neurologist. Smoking pot in my bedroom. Feeling sorry for myself. Having seizures. Life was complete shit again.

Chapter 9 - Seizures Are Not Good for Girlfriends

My sister called a couple of days later. She herself was very sick. She has Ulcerative Colitis and things had reached the point where she needed help. She would probably need hospitalization soon. Her husband is a Marine, he was in Okinawa at the time, and she was hoping I could come out to California and help her for a little while. Maybe like her live-in nurse.

It sounded like a shitty job. It wasn't even a job – there was no money in it. It sounded depressing and yet it seemed like a pretty damn good idea.

Hell, being in a position to help my sister was probably the one good thing that came out of all the bad things that happened in my life at that time.

At the time, my sister lived in Twenty Nine Palms in the middle of the high desert. There was nothing to do except play chess, take care of my sister, and think about what I should do next with my life. It was horribly depressing and the fact that my sister was in and out of the hospital at the time didn't help.

The woman I was dating at the time wanted to come out to visit. It seemed like a really bad idea. The house was small and my sister didn't know her. I was always in a crappy mood and falling down a lot. Between the fact that I was grumpy and no longer on the road and coming by her house anymore, our relationship soon ended. Seizures aren't good for girlfriends, either.

I stayed busy. I was my sister's "nurse." I had duties. I made breakfast. I brought her her medication. I had to help clean her up now and then. She has Ulcerative Colitis so feces came into play more than once. And I had a lot of time to do nothing except sit and think about how shitty (no pun intended) my life had become. And think about how something had to change. Finally, I figured out what I had to do. I had to move.

I couldn't work in Detroit. There just wasn't enough work in the local comedy clubs to sustain me. One psychopathic booking agent ran all the clubs and even that required a lot of driving around town. Also, he didn't pay very well. To work Detroit would also mean finding a day-job. While I had no problem with that, again it would have meant more driving.

Also, everyone in the comedy business in Detroit was well aware of my situation. I needed to go someplace where no one knew I had seizures.

I avoided looking at my friends and family after a seizure. While this was never a conscious thought, I knew it crossed my mind many times. Sort of, "Never ever let them see you fall down." Somehow there was this thought in my mind that anyone who saw me fall would never take me seriously again. I would be, to them, some sort of freak. So I needed to isolate myself in those situations as best I could. Of course, I couldn't isolate my seizures so I isolated myself. It seemed like an intelligent approach at the time.

But where to move?

I thought about Los Angeles. Nope. That was no good. Too crowded and too expensive. Plus, I really don't like the scene there. Phony people convinced that the whole world, if they could afford it, would live in La-La Land. People who smile while they shit on you – and then stick their wallets in your mouth when you have a seizure just to show they really care -- didn't seem like a good place to cheer up.

Chicago? Not enough paying work for a guy like me with no car.

New York? I hate New York. The food is good and they have an amazing subway system (good for someone who is trying to avoid driving), but I didn't really know anybody in New York and it costs more to live there than in Los Angeles. Plus it's dirty and cold. I had no money and I wanted someplace warm with actual paying work. Dangling the prospect of maybe "making it big" someday to get me to work for free today didn't really entice me. No, New York was out.

Then I thought about Orlando, Florida. I knew people down there, the weather was nice and the living was relatively cheap. There was plenty of work and plenty to do. Granted, much of the work sucked and paid shitty, but at least there was lots of it -- without having to drive all over the state.

I also liked the fact that it was a twenty-two hour drive from my family. The "pop-in" seemed unlikely. Yes, Orlando was a winner.

I have to admit, if you are going to be depressed, do it somewhere warm. Do it somewhere cheap. Do it somewhere with an amusement park. It really helps. When I left the California desert, I moved to Orlando and the next stage of my life. I was still depressed but at least I had distractions.

Chapter 10 - I Prefer Falling Down Alone

When you get right down to it, half of the time there is no story to a seizure. One moment you are standing there, and the next moment you are laying there. Personally, I prefer falling down alone. No one saw it and you don't remember it. Game over.

Well, almost over.

If you are lucky, you are laying somewhere comfortable. You were close enough to a sofa or a chair or a bed and you got there. Or maybe you hit the floor but got to a soft piece of carpet. Maybe you even got a pillow under your head. There isn't any blood. You didn't hit your head or your arm or your back on the way down. That's always nice.

If you were not quite so lucky, you have to change clothes. Let's be honest, pissing your pants is not the end of the world. And if you do have to change clothes, it's always better when that happens in the privacy of your own space. For me, that is always more annoying when it happens in public. People can be as nice and helpful as they want; it doesn't alter the fact that I don't want to talk to anyone when I am dripping wet with my own bodily fluids.

If you were unlucky when it happened, then you are somewhere not so comfy. I used to have seizures in the shower all the time. I have been told this is fairly common. While it came with the advantage of making it easier to clean myself up, it had the disadvantage of being horribly uncomfortable. Waking up with your face pressed against that shower wall is never good, and for some reason the positions I ended up in were always terrible. It also often meant I hit things like the faucet the soap dish or the edge of the tub on the way down. I have more than a few scars from shower incidents.

At least if you are alone, you can take a few moments to recover. No one is around. I always seem to need sleep after a seizure. To this day, I set alarms all day for when I need to be places or do things. It is a habit I got into when I was having a lot of seizures. I never knew when I would have a seizure and need a nap – and need to be woken up to go to work.

Whatever the case, I always took solace in the fact that at least I was alone. As far as the rest of the world was concerned, I was having a normal day, just like them. Maybe that is a terrible way to live. Maybe that is some sort of defense mechanism. But what am I supposed to do? Shout to the world, "I just had a seizure! Woo Hoo!"

No. I get up, keep it to myself, and move on with my life. Having it alone made this much easier than having it on the fifty-yard line at a football game.

I was having most of my seizures alone when I was living in Florida. I had rented a room from two friends of mine in Orlando and I lived there for several years. At first, I had precious little comedy work and had to take some side jobs to make ends meet.

I tried to get a job at Disney World, but the seizure thing made my options there limited (Disney is "nice" about hiring people like me but they have very limited choices about what jobs are available.) I ended up working at a pizza shop near Disney off and on for the first year. They were nice people and they treated me well.

But I was having plenty of seizures.

I got into jogging while in Florida. Karl, my roommate, had a big husky named "Rama." I used to take the dog with me because the dog would keep up with me. I never used a leash. I just ran out the front door and the dog never left my side.

For some reason, I started having seizures almost every time I ran. It started to drive me nuts. It made me not want to stay in shape. But I fought it and kept on running.

The last time I ran, I took off out the front door. The neighborhood was new and still mostly under construction. Rama and I headed towards the back of the development where all of the houses were still just frames.

I don't remember going down. But I certainly remember getting up. I was face down in the ground of a new home under construction. I remember lifting my head, with the dirt falling away from my face. Rama started licking my face. I turned over on my back. A huge construction worker blocked out the sun. It was really hot and I couldn't see him very well.

"I thought you were dead," he said bluntly.

"I'm OK," I replied. But I wasn't really moving yet.

"I saw you from over there. I saw you go down. I thought sure you had a heart attack."

"No. I'm OK. Thanks." I stood up. I felt a little shaky. Rama was still licking me.

"You sure? I thought for sure you were dead," he said again.

"No. I'm fine. Really. I appreciate it." With that, I turned and tried to start running again. In truth, it was more of a walk.

"Man, you OK?" he called after me. "You need a ride or something?"

"No. I live right around the corner. Thanks!"

I remember thinking about how it must have looked from his perspective. It must have been weird. But I didn't want to stand there and talk about it. I wanted to go home and take a shower. To this day I have not gotten back into running. Twice, I have purchased new running shoes. Twice, I have done the "first day." But I haven't managed to become a runner again. I don't know if it's too painful or the memories of that seizure are too strong.

There is something about all those things that remind you of seizures. I can't watch TV shows that were on when I was having a seizure. Certain songs remind me of seizures. I was wearing CK1 Cologne for about a year when I had a lot of them and the smell of it still makes me sick. I can't stand to be around anyone who is wearing it. Whenever anything reminds me of a seizure, I have a physical feeling that I need to get away. Sometimes, I even need to avoid people who have been around me when I have had a seizure.

Chapter 11 - Casinos Can Be a Crapshoot

I started doing comedy in casinos around the country. I'm a comedian. We know how to find work. It was a nice gig. I would live in the casino for a month or two, sometimes even three months at a time. No one that I know saw me and I worked a lot. The money sucked but I didn't spend much. I had a lot of seizures but no one that I know saw them. I felt like I managed to get a certain amount of control over things. I drank, smoked a lot of pot, wrote a lot, and became a much better comedian, thanks to a great work schedule. And while I still had to drive occasionally, I only had to drive to get to the casino. Once I was there, I could park my car and not touch it again for months.

I thought I had found the perfect job. I was wrong.

Casinos were great for what they were. I always knew that it was not going to be a career job, but I really did enjoy them. In five years working casinos, I only made one true friend: A hotel manager from Rhode Island named Mike. We used play Golden Tee all night. We used to go golfing on his day off. We used to drive up to Memphis and eat pulled pork.

But casinos were a strange place. I was alone and bored. I did strange things to kill the time. I shaved my testicles. I learned to juggle. I learned to wire a television so I could steal the payperview movies. And I wrote. I wrote two really bad screenplays. I burned both of them.

I wrote a lot of jokes. I wrote music. I wrote poetry. I wrote anything I could come up with that would kill the time. I wrote, quite literally, for months on end.

I made almost no money and did my best to spend as little of that as possible. It was not easy. And I tried to stay in my hotel room as much as possible because I was having more and more seizures.

Eventually, I stayed in my room and simply went out to perform and to eat. But even that couldn't guarantee that I would never have a seizure in public.

I was eating lunch one day at the Imperial Palace in Biloxi, Mississippi. It was the buffet and there were about fifty people enjoying the standard fare of potato salad and roast beef. I am not sure if I knew I was about to have a seizure or if I just got confused. I don't really remember what I was thinking.

But I do remember getting up from the table and walking to the section of the dining room where no people were seated. I remember looking for an area where no one could see me and being horribly panicked by the fact that people could still see me. I walked from table to table looking for a place where I could be unobserved. I like to think that I was looking for some privacy to have a seizure, but I have to admit, from the memories I have of the seizures I remember, and these are the less intense seizures, that I rarely have that much clarity. In reality, I was probably avoiding some fifth- grade teacher or "Robocop."

But you never know. I just might have been looking for a place to lie down.

Whatever the case, I didn't make it. I fell face down in between a couple tables right in front of a bunch of people. For some reason, I had decided to head out of the restaurant and so I was at the most crowded point of the dining room when I went down.

At least that was where I woke up. With security, some paramedics, and a whole slew of people standing over me.

Because I was working as a comedian in that casino, I had to fill out a security report. The hotel manager called me into his office and asked me a bunch of questions. It was clear that he believed I was some sort of a drug addict. I told him I was not. I did not tell him I had a pocket full of marijuana.

I talked to the manager and after a brief conversation everything calmed down. But it was horribly embarrassing. I assured him that these sorts of seizures were terribly rare – which was, at that time, a significant lie. I was having several a week. Luckily for me, the vast majority were occurring in private. It was very rare for anything to occur in public.

But this week was going to be one of those times. I was in my room one afternoon. I was taking a shower. Out of nowhere I went down. I have no recollection of anything. I just woke up on the floor.

It sounds funny to people who don't have them, but I prefer Grand Mal seizures to Petite Mal seizures. Grand Mal are the big ones. The ones where you flop around the floor and look horrible. Petite Mal are the ones where you, the audience, see virtually nothing.

From my perspective, during a Grand Mal: One minute I am standing there and the next I am somewhere else. During a Petite Mal I remember the panic, the thrashing, and the desperate clawing to escape the dark well that I have somehow fallen into. I get to enjoy all of it. Which really sucks.

The only real problem with the Grand Mal is the waking up from them.

I opened my eyes. The floor was cold tile. I realized I was naked. I laid there for several seconds before I moved. I kept taking in all my senses. I was very sore, like I had been lifting weights all day. I went ahead and lifted myself up anyway.

As I lifted myself up, my head started to throb. Not like a headache but a very specific pounding in the back of my head. It felt like someone had ground a stone into my head and was pushing it into my skull. It hurt that bad.

I stood up. The shower was still running. I was wet and the bathroom was steamy.

I turned off the water and walked out into the bedroom. I was tired and dizzy. I had to lie down. I sprawled across the bed and fell asleep almost immediately. I have very few seizures where I don't sleep afterwards.

My alarm went off at 7:00 p.m. I always set my alarm several times a day to remind myself of the things I have to do. It helps keep me from being late. My first show was at 8:00 p.m. I never know when I am going to take a nap or be on the phone so I always set an alarm. This was a good example of why.

I turned the alarm off and tried to lift my head. It was very difficult. I was stuck to the pillow. When I pulled my head off and looked, I realized the pillow was covered in blood. The pillow and sheet under it looked like I had stabbed someone to death.

I walked into the bathroom. There was a good-sized pool of blood in there, too.

I touched my head. It hurt bad – and, surprisingly, it was still bleeding.

But I had to do the show. I got dressed, put a washcloth on my head and put a baseball hat over it. I walked down to the showroom.

It was a two-man show. I open the show, the other comic closes, and I do the final bit to end the evening. I didn't really like the other comic, although that was nothing new. I figured I would just do my thing and get some sleep. Things would be better in the morning.

But my head really hurt now. I was light headed and I was pretty sure I was still bleeding. I didn't know what time the seizure had happened and I didn't know how long my head had been bleeding.

Furthermore, I was getting confused. I knew that wasn't a good sign.

I started my show. I had a hard time concentrating. I could feel the blood dripping down the back of my neck. I checked it with my hand and saw red on my fingers. Still bleeding after all this time? I realized I couldn't wait for another hour for the show to be over before I did something about it.

I introduced the next act. As our paths crossed on stage, I quickly, quietly told him he would have to take himself off at the end of his show. I wasn't going to stick around to close out the performance.

"You're going to have to take yourself off," I said in my best stage whisper. "What?" he responded. "You serious?" I showed him my fingers. They were red with rich, thick blood. "Yeah. OK. Sure," he said, giving me a curious worried look.

I have no idea what happened to the rest of the show. I left and drove myself to the hospital where I got eight stitches in my head. I did the next night's show wearing a baseball cap. I thought that was appropriate.

Despite the collapse at the buffet and taking the stage with a bloody washcloth stuck to my head, I continued to work long-term casino gigs for almost three years. Even more surprising to me than holding this job for so long, is that when it ended, it had nothing to do with a seizure.

Chapter 12 – The End Of An Era

It's a twelve-hour drive from my home in Florida to Tunica, Mississippi. Like I said before, I only had to drive once every couple months so by then I felt pretty confident about the driving part. I made sure to get plenty of sleep, eat right, and be ready for the drives when they came. I knew I shouldn't drive. But only driving once every couple months seemed OK.

It was about eleven o'clock on a cool spring morning. The road was clear and the weather was great. It was my birthday.

I had decided to take state roads to make the drive a little more interesting. I was in the middle of nowhere in Georgia. Not a cloud in the sky or a car in sight. One moment I was clipping along at sixty miles per hour and the next...!

Getting into a serious accident is a weird thing. I have been in several but this was one of my strangest. I remember almost all of it.

I was driving my alltime favorite road car; a red 1995 four-door Chevy Cavalier. I have had three Cavaliers in my life, and they all ran amazingly well. I put three hundred thousand miles on the first one before I cracked the engine block and sold it for four hundred dollars and walked home from the garage. It had never been in the shop. I put fifty thousand miles on the last one before I moved to England and sold the car, for obvious reasons. This was the middle one, and it had a hundred and fifty thousand miles on it at the time. I considered it in perfect condition.

I kept a cooler on the floor in front of the passenger seat. I kept writing paraphernalia on the passenger seat. I had snacks on the floor behind me and a pilfered hotel room wastebasket behind the passenger seat. The trunk was filled with movies, food, clothes, and my guitar – everything I would need for a couple of months in a casino. It was amazing. Even the seat had become perfectly molded to fit my ass.

I was near Donalsonville, Georgia, where they had had a lot of rain in recent weeks. The road was dry, but the shoulders were very muddy. There was standing water everywhere along the sides of the road.

My car hit a rut in the road and lurched to the shoulder. It hit the mud on the shoulder and the car lurched to the right. When I jerked it back on the road, it started to slide to the left. I was used to driving on ice from my youth so I didn't panic. I drove the car to straighten it out. But it didn't straighten out. The car just started sliding like I was on ice. I learned later that the tires were probably covered with mud.

The car continued to slide very fast and drifted off the road. I watched out the driver's side window at what looked like a lake coming hurtling toward me. It turned out to be a large pool of standing water. I said out loud, "This isn't going to be good."

I don't remember the car hitting the water. I don't remember any impact. The cop who did the investigation told me that I flipped the car. I find that hard to believe, but I know I hit my head, so who's to say?

The next thing I knew, I was sitting behind the wheel, looking back at the road. There was this weird kind of silence except for the sound of the engine running. I could see that my car was mostly under water. I knew that this was not where I wanted to be. I stepped on the gas to try to drive the car back to the road. The engine stopped.

I looked to my right. That was an old habit. On the highway, every time I jammed on my brakes, my tapes and personal stuff went flying off the seat so I would always check to see if they needed sorting. Now, I saw much of my precious stuff floating about breast high in muddy water. Again, not good.

I looked to my left. The driver's side door was gone and a lot of my belongings were floating in the water outside the car.

I moved to get out of the car. I was, of course, still wearing my seatbelt. I felt like an idiot from some bad comedy show, but no one was around, so I ignored it. I took my seat belt off and waded to the shore. Dripping water and mud, I sat down on the side of the road and stared at my car. Only the windshield and a little of the hood were now sticking out of the water. I just sat there. And stared. And thought about – nothing, really. I just sat there. I think I was in a little bit of shock.

No cars came driving by. There were no sounds. There was just my car and me for about ten minutes. I didn't really have anything floating through my head except, "Shit!"

I looked at the items floating nearby in the water. I saw my tapes, I saw a couple pieces of my clothing, and I saw my papers. I saw my wallet. I thought "Well, I'm gonna need that stuff." So I got back in the water and retrieved as much as I could carry.

Once I was in the water, I started gathering up the rest of my stuff. I started throwing things onto the shore.

I felt my iron on the bottom of the pond. I went under and got it. I grabbed everything I could get my hands on.

A car drove by and asked if I was OK. I told them I was. A cop showed up about fifteen minutes later. We talked for about ten minutes and then he did a little investigation. He found, through my brake marks, that I was not speeding and, after discovering the rut, that the road had, indeed, caused the accident.

We stood there talking for an hour or so while we waited for the tow truck. I felt kind of bad for the tow truck guy, because he had to go under the water to hook up my car. But what can you do? That's where my car was.

The one thing the cop did tell me was that the seatbelt probably saved my life. He said that in this type of accident, I certainly would have been thrown from the car without it. He said that maybe I would have lived, but I certainly would not be standing there talking to him. We would be at the hospital.

I got towed into the nearby metropolis of Donalsonville.

A really nice mechanic took pity on me and drove me to his own house. We fed his horses while they worked on my car. He said that he wouldn't know about the car for days. I told him that I needed to get to my gig at the casino. And I asked him, just between us men, was the car totaled?

"Yup," he said, without hesitating. "Water over the dashboard. That car ain't never running again." "When does the next bus come through?" I asked. "Thursday," he said. This was on Monday.

"Where is the nearest airport?" I inquired. "Dothan, Alabama," he answered.

"How far is that?" "About an hour." "Where can I rent a car?"

"Dothan."

"What are my options?"

"Wait until Thursday."

"Or?"

"Or a week from Thursday," he said.

I sat in the auto repair shop and had lunch. They really were nice people. Just the old man and his wife. They weren't trying to be mean or mess with the Yankee. I was just kind of screwed.

An hour later, the old man came out and told me that he would drive me to Dothan. And he refused to accept any money for gas, no matter how many times I offered. He actually felt bad that all this had happened to me.

He dropped me off at the airport.

Of course, the way my luck was running, my flight to Memphis was delayed and later cancelled so I spent the night at the Ramada Inn in Dothan, Alabama. I wish I could say it was the worst hotel I have ever stayed in, but, unfortunately, I am a comic who has worked the road. Comedy clubs put you up in some pretty nasty places.

I called my parents but they were out of town. I called my sister but she was gone. I started calling everyone I knew, more than anything to convince myself that this nightmare was really happening to me. I finally got a hold of a friend from college. He laughed.

I ate dinner at Denny's. Shortly before midnight, I ordered a chocolate shake to celebrate my birthday. They were all out of chocolate. "Of course you are," I told the guy behind the counter.

I got a call at my hotel at 5:00 a.m. It was from the airline agent who had sent me to the hotel from the airport. He was calling to tell me that the airline had me booked on a flight at 1:00 p.m. – but that 1 o'clock flight was going to be cancelled. If I wanted to wait, they would rebook me on a flight that was scheduled to leave at 8:00 p.m. But that would mean I would miss my show at the casino. If I wanted to make it to Memphis in time for work, I needed to get up now and get back to the airport immediately.

I couldn't make this stuff up. I jumped out of bed and caught the hotel shuttle to the airport.

I made it to the casino – still in wet clothes from my accident, reeking of mud, oil, horsefeed and whatever else I had picked up in the previous thirty-six hours.

But anyway, I made it. I did the gig. I looked horrible and smelled worse but I got paid. I called my father and had him buy me another car.

Actually, I paid for it. I called the dealership where a friend of mine from high school worked and I did all the paperwork over the phone. I got the same car, same make, same model. I had my dad pick the car up and drive it to me in Memphis, along with some more clothes.

When my father showed up in Memphis with my new car, it was perfect. It was dark green and sat a little lower than the last one (I should have gotten the fourdoor again. I don't know why I didn't). It was never quite as tasty as the red one, but it was pretty good.

Now, I know this story didn't actually transpire because of a seizure. But, sitting there in the silence on the side of the road, looking at my car in the muddy water, I realized something: I had had several serious accidents in a short period of time. Several were caused by my own stupidity. I cannot even legally drive. There is probably a good reason for that and I was living it. If I don't get out of the car immediately, I told myself, I am going to die.

So I did. I finished the gig and went home. I never worked casinos again. Once again, my life was over. I needed to start all over again.

Chapter 13 - Welcome Aboard

The night I had had the car accident in Oklahoma City, the horrible incident involving the motorcycle, and the little girl, I sat in the bar at the Comedy Club, got drunk and talked to the other comedian. His name is Carl Faulkenberry. A very nice guy whom I really didn't know that well at the time. Nonetheless I spilled my guts to him because that's the way comics are.

Carl asked me, "Why don't you work cruise ships?"

I had never given them much thought before. Cruise ships were considered the pariahs of the comedy industry. First of all, there is no chance of advancement when you work in the middle of the ocean. Who is going to see you? No agents, no bookers, no auditions. It is a professional dead end.

Secondly, it was "well known" that the "bosses" onboard stole all of your material. Worse still, the people in the corporate offices didn't care. The "Cruise Directors" were free to steal your material and then fire you, if they saw fit, on a whim. They could then do your act at their discretion.

Thirdly, the material a comedian can get away with onboard cruise ships is tricky at best. There are kids in the audience. The adults themselves are on vacation and do not pay for tickets to the show. They are a demanding and opinionated audience that, as a whole, views the entertainment onboard as something they are "owed." They complain vociferously if anything is not exactly what they want or believe they deserve.   They are an incredibly diverse group that loves you one week, and hates you the next. And the cruise companies are obsessed with keeping their customers happy. You have to work clean, fast and furious. And any show that is not fantastic can mean your termination.

At least those were the prevailing views of cruise ships among casino and club comics. I had heard the whole litany many times.

On the plus side, as I soon discovered, the pay on cruise lines is decent. They even pay for your plane tickets and cabs to and from the ship. No more having to drive cross country, on your own dime, to get to work. They pay for your food and lodging while you are onboard and the people who work there are generally very nice. The "mean" Cruise Directors are, in reality, few and far between. The audiences are, in fact, as receptive as any other.

I remembered what Carl had told me. Cruise ships kind of dangled out there in the ether as some sort of magical place that I might eventually end up. After the accident in Georgia, I contacted a cruise agency. I needed to stop driving. My seizures were not getting any better. To my surprise, I was hired almost immediately and sent to Barbados to get on a ship.

It was massive. Thirty-five hundred guests. Fifteen hundred crew. A seven or eight-story building, three or four football fields long. Twelve decks above the water line. And just this little hole in the side to get into the ship. When I walked up to the ship to sign on, I was awestruck. It was just me and some guy standing there at the end of the gangway saying, "Welcome aboard." It was terribly intimidating.

I signed on with a juggler named Manuel Zuniga, who has since become one of my best friends. He was very nice and showed me around on my first day. My cabin was small but clean and had everything I needed. Everybody onboard was nice. Too nice. Much nicer than most people treated me in the clubs and casinos. It was fantastic.

The work took a little getting used to. I was not prepared to have both five-year olds and eighty-year olds in the front row. Some of my best jokes fell on deaf ears. Some of what were my weakest jokes in casinos and clubs turned out to be my best ones aboard cruise ships. I had to move the order around and write some new material quickly. It wasn't that hard, though. After about a month, I had the gig figured out.

People always ask me if I have ever had a seizure onstage. I had my first one almost immediately after going to work for the cruise line.

I often have no memory of the time before the seizure but I almost always remember the instant I wake up. This was one of those seizures. All I remember is waking up on the floor in front of 1,200 people who were silently staring at me. I had no idea what jokes I had told, or how long I had been laying there. All I knew was that 1,200 people were staring at me.

I always am a little out of it for a couple seconds when I wake up. I am not sure how bad it was. Have I been out a long time? No. It couldn't have been too long. They wouldn't all still be sitting there. Would they? Would someone have done something?

Or have I done something horrible. Have I been flopping around the floor, foaming at the mouth, shouting obscenities, "Fuck this, fuckers! RAR! RAAAR!"

No. That doesn't seem right either. I don't think I've pissed myself. But I don't want to go right for the crotch, though. What could I do?

I jumped up. Actually, "jumped" is probably an exaggeration. I got up, and said. "Well, now that that's over . . . " A couple of people in the audience laughed.

I have a nice eight-minute closing bit with a ukulele and I know I haven't gotten to it yet because the ukulele itself is still backstage. So I go right to the ukulele. I didn't even make a joke about the seizure. What could I say? And quite frankly, at that point in my life, I wasn't comfortable enough about it to tell jokes about it. I have since gotten over that and talk about it in every show. But at that time, I was very self-conscious about it all and the last thing I wanted to do was to start talking about epilepsy onstage.

I was still kind of shaking, so the ukulele bit wasn't very good. I was never very good at playing it, anyway. But it worked. I got through it and got off the stage.

The cruise director, my boss, and the emcee of the show, looked like he was going to vomit when I got backstage. He just said, "I didn't know what to do."

I said, "Well, now you do." He said, "What?"

I said, "Nothing. When I have a seizure, I'll do all the work."

Of course, I was upset. I thought to myself, "So you just let me lay there? Flopping around the floor? What the fuck is wrong with you?" But the man was my boss and I was new to ships. This horrible line was my best attempt at a joke to make him feel better about the way he had handled the situation. Which is to say, his utter lack of handling the situation. But it didn't really affect anything. As long as he was happy or at least not going to fire me.

Chapter 14 - "Love Boat" It Isn't

I took a position with the cruise line as a "live on" act, which meant I would stay on the ship for months on end, further limiting my time in the car. It took some getting used to, but I was free to hide in my cabin and be depressed. No one knew me, so no one even knew how depressed I was. And everyone else seemed to have some issue that had brought him or her to ships in the first place. So, interestingly enough, I fit right in.

I was quietly trying to progress with my life when I met the ship's doctor. He was an evil son of a bitch from Germany. I not-so-affectionately called him "Mengele" and he fired me several time because he thought a man with seizures should not work aboard a ship. He was convinced that I would have a seizure and fall overboard.

He made me report to him every time the ship got to the homeport to be "inspected for bruises." I have seizures so I have bruises. Big surprise.

But the little Nazi took great pleasure, it seemed, in rubbing his fingers through my hair, and in massaging my legs -- all in the name of "protecting my medical interest." And yet, in the beginning, every couple weeks he would "find something" and terminate my employment. And, man, I needed that job.

Luckily for me, the vice president of the cruise line was much more understanding and would override the doctor's authority. But that only made "Mengele" more upset.

He would lecture me: "You think you are so smart," and "I am only concerned with your best interest." And the inspections would continue.

The inspections finally ended one day when he was busy and decided to do his bruise inspection in the crew common room. There, in front of several other crew members, he started to check me out. I, being the big mouth that I am, started calling him some very unflattering names, referencing the worst in German World War II history.

He pulled my pants down (In frustration, I assume, over not being shown the respect he felt he deserved) and started examining my genitals – again, in full view of everyone in the room.

I started calling him, very quietly, every slur for a homosexual and a Nazi that I could think of. "Enjoy yourself," I said. "Because this is the last time I will ever be in your infirmary." "If you wish to work here, you will do what you are told," he fired back. He pulled my pants up and I left. I went directly to the cruise director's office and called the cruise line's home offices in Miami. Again, the vice president was very kind and understanding.

The next day I was called to the Hotel Directors office. Next to the Captain, the Hotel Director is the highest-ranking person on a cruise ship. There I was told I did not ever have to go the infirmary again.

I only wish I could say seizures caused me no more problems, but they did. I was having them pretty regularly on that ship. To the point where, for the first time in my life, my friends were becoming comfortable with it.

The music director would see the crowd around me (which Is inevitable when you have a seizure in public) and he would walk up, grab my wallet, and steal $20. He then would slam the wallet on the floor and say, "I told you I would get that money from you eventually!" and leave before I would wake up. The crowd would, of course, be horrified.

If I had a seizure in my cabin, another friend of mine would just step over me, take a beer from my refrigerator, and walk out. The effect was fantastic because everyone would talk about how heartless he was. Did he not notice the man flopping on the floor?

It wasn't all great. There were drills. There were inspections. Ships can be a rude awakening for a comedian accustomed to the laid-back life in comedy clubs.

My awakening happened during a standard security inspection one morning. I was still asleep when security knocked on my cabin door. "Security!" The security guards on our ships were mostly from India and usually pretty nice guys. They always announced themselves when they knocked on your door. Even when they were off duty. Habits die hard, I suppose, and a guy coming by to watch the game on television would still announce himself at your door. Or maybe they thought it was funny.

I opened my cabin door to find the Assistant Chief of Security standing there with one of his assistants. It was policy for someone from my department to be there as well, but none was there that particular morning. It didn't really bother me. The Assistant Chief and I had been friends since we discovered we both liked college basketball. His cabin was a couple doors away from mine and we would sit outside of our respective cabins and yell obscenities at each other as the games progressed. Probably due to our friendship, he never really made an issue during inspections of my microwave, the large amounts of food in my cabin, or the George Forman Grill I used nightly – all of which were against company policy. He would usually just stand in the doorway and announce, "Cabin 271, fine."

Anyway, on this particular morning, I stood in the doorway in my boxer briefs and said "Hey, Rik, c'mon in."
His name was not Rik but I always had a hard time pronouncing his given Indian name. In retrospect, he probably didn't like it at all and I probably should have taken the time to learn the pronunciation. Not much I can do about it now.

"I will return when you collect yourself." Rik said, as he took a long drag on his cigarette and stared me right in the eye. This was 2002, after all. People could still smoke wherever they wanted.

I was a little confused. I had certainly answered the door in my underwear before. We worked different schedules and he knew I didn't care if he woke me up. For that matter, he knew all I was going to do when he left was go back to bed.

"Rik. Dude. Do your thing. It's cool." Maybe just calling him "dude" was not enough to tell him I was fine with him waking me up. I turned the light on in my cabin – revealing the microwave, plug-in air freshener, and mass amount of food, not to mention a full case of empty beer cans. From a security perspective, my cabin was not exactly "minty fresh."

Rik's eyes never left mine. "Collect yourself. I will return in 30 minutes."

I glanced around the room. Maybe he was doing me a favor and trying to tell me to hide something. But I couldn't see anything. There was nothing wrong with my cabin that hadn't been wrong during the last twenty inspections.

"Rik, man. What's the problem? C'mon in. Do what you gotta do." If I was going to get a warning, I was going to get it eventually anyway. Besides, getting a warning was akin to getting sent to the principal's office. It meant nothing. No one got fired for a written warning. No one got fired for two. Hell, unless you really screwed up, I have never known anyone to get fired even after piles of written warnings. They are meaningless.

"Collect yourself. I will be back in 30 minutes," he said again He took a long drag on his cigarette and his eyes tore into my skull. His assistant just laughed and they walked away.

I closed the door and turned the light off. As I lay back down onto my bed I thought about what could have been bothering Rik. And then it came to me. Or rather, I noticed it.

Poking through my shorts was a raging erection. I had had the entire exchange with my penis fully erect and poking through my underwear. A large Indian man had seen my penis. Well, at least he had paid me the courtesy of not staring at it. But maybe that had only made it worse. What's wrong with my pecker, anyway?

Chapter 15 - Be Careful When You Call Someone a Nazi

Life went on, and, a few years later, I was leaving town, leaving the country, actually, so I was driving to the airport. To be honest, I knew better. But I hadn't had a seizure in about a year and in some states (though not the one I was in) a year without a seizure is all you need to drive legally. There was a lot of traffic and it wasn't moving. We were inching along. Twenty feet, stop. Thirty feet, stop.

All of a sudden, I woke up and my car was pulled over to the side of the road. I don't remember pulling off the road, but thank God I had the clarity of mind to do that. Now I was sitting on the ground, next to the car. My car's engine was still running and the driver's side door was open. I had no memory of getting out of the car either. I sat there for a minute and let my head clear. I was a little confused, but at that point I was getting used to those things. I was more embarrassed at having been behind the wheel. I mean, Jesus! I thought I was controlled at this point.

Then I looked up and saw a cop car speeding toward me. Instantly, I knew I was going to jail. After all, I am a seizure patient. It is illegal for me to drive and I know it. Yet here I am. And I just had a seizure. Shit, shit, shit.

The cop was young and really didn't really know what to do. He asked a lot of questions and had clearly called an ambulance. I was very tragically honest with him. No, I didn't do any drugs. Honest. Yes, he can test me for drugs. No, I didn't have a lot to drink the night before. I had had one beer. I never drink much when I have to get up early to fly. It gives me a headache and I'm too old for the whole "hung-over flight" thing. Yes, he can test. No, I'm not lying.

He still didn't know what to do. Sure I could have helped. I could have told him not to let me drive. But that's like admitting to the principal or your girlfriend all the crappy things you have done. Always keep your mouth shut. Never confess.

The ambulance arrived and checked me out. They didn't do any tests. They talked to me for a couple minutes and I heard the paramedic say to the policeman, "He's not on anything."

So the cop let me go.

I made my plane. I was flying to Italy and had to change plane in Geneva, Switzerland. The woman at the Air Berlin ticket counter told me that my bag was too big to carry on; she said it had to be checked. I told her that would be fine. I asked her to wait one moment so that I could take out my medication, just in case the bag was lost.

She asked me what the medication was for.

I told her.

She asked if I had any sort of documentation to prove that I was, in fact, epileptic. Had I really thought about it, I still had the police report from that morning, but I was still kind of hazy.

I said I did not. I told her that we didn't do anything like that in the United States. She snapped, "The entire civilized world has cards for things like that. If you were really epileptic, you would have a card." I said, 'I would think the medication itself would be proof. It's not like anti-convulsants have a street-value." "Why don't you Americans just do what you're told?" she shot back "I don't know why you're making this personal," I said. "If I wanted to reach into my bag and take out a book, wouldn't I be able to?" "Just leave the bag. Go to your plane. When you get to Italy you can pick it up." "I would feel a lot better if I had my medication." "How do I know you are really epileptic?" "How about I fall on the floor and piss myself right here?" "Why are you Americans always so difficult?" "Why did you people fund the Germans in World War II?"

That was really my mistake. I was upset. I was in another country. I had no idea why this woman was yelling at me. Calling her a Nazi really didn't help my situation any -- although it did make me think that I had some fixation with Germans, or maybe I just watch too much of the History Channel.

She threw my bag against the wall, banging my computer – which still has a dent – and breaking several items. Mercifully, the bag and the medication made it to Italy. But I never did find out if the Swiss really have cards for seizure patients.

Chapter 16   There Is Love At Sea After All

I was decidedly not dating at that time. I had no interest in women. I wanted to spend my time alone and be dark and bitter in my own little angry world. I listened to angry music and dressed in black clothes with a leather bracelet. I drank too much. I swore a lot. I yelled a lot. I was not a nice person.

However, eventually I did go back to see the ship's doctor again. They had gotten rid of the German and this lovely woman was there now. Samantha Trevinia Claire Digby. Such an English name.

She was this funny, smart, beautiful, delightful woman from England. Even her accent made me smile. I can't say it was love at first sight, because I was too angry to even see her at first, but I fell in love for the first time in my life very quickly.

Don't get me wrong, I thought I was in love before. And I certainly have told women I loved them, usually to enhance my chances of getting them to do something they didn't want to do. But with this woman it was different. I knew it right away. And, two kids later, I still like talking about it. I still like emailing her in the middle of the night. When I am gone for two days, I call her -- not because she expects it, which she doesn't. She is usually annoyed because I break into her "wii" time. But I call because I genuinely want to talk to her.

No, this time I really fell in love. And it was great.

The first thing that made me notice that Sam was different than most women I knew was a bet we made.

At the time, the cruise line had a card that all crewmembers were required to carry. The card had company vernacular on it that crew members were required to use. "Official Company Phrases." Things like "My Pleasure," not "No Problem." I was completely against the card because I believe that personal character means everything. Why, for example, hire a man from Jamaica and then tell him that his national motto is unwelcome?

OK, I admit it. I was being silly. I was still an angry guy and I was against everything that I could come up with a reason for being against. The card was fine. The company had a point and was simply trying to start coming up with "Corporate standards." But I had chosen something silly and stupid to vent my anger about seizures on.

Sam pulled out the card in the crew bar one night and I gave her a lot of grief about it. I told her I would piss on the card and she bet me $100 that I wouldn't. The rules were established that I could ask for the card at any time as long as I did it in public.

The first time I tried, she beat me. She said, "Look, It was a silly bet. All my phone numbers are on it. Forget the whole thing." I felt bad. I gave her back the card.

She put it in her wallet and laughed in my face and said, "You're an amateur. You will never win this bet." You had to respect that.

However, she clearly had no idea what a comedian is capable of. We were at the Captain's dinner a couple days later. Everyone was dressed in tuxedos. There was fine china on the table. I told her "Give me the card."

She said, "No. No, no no. You can't do that here. We will get in trouble." Trouble? I like that.

I smiled and nodded. The only person on board who knew about the bet was our friend, Junior Powell, the Food and Beverage Manager from Jamaica. He chuckled.

She refused and I let her off the hook. Until that night in the crew bar where I dropped the card under the table, whipped out my wiener, and dropped a stream right across the card.

The next morning at the Captain's meeting, a very serious meeting with all the senior officers, most of whom are in their 50's and from Italy, I announced, "Before we get started, the doctor owes me a hundred dollars."

Junior chimed in "Tell them why, Doctor. Announce to everyone why you are giving the comedian money."

Sam, of course, said nothing. She just gave me my hundred dollars. We have been together ever since.

I bring this all up because she has had a profound effect on my life. I found that almost immediately after meeting Sam, I relaxed. Slowly, over time, my demeanor changed. My whole body unclenched. I slept better. My stress level went down. I dealt with things better.

I started having fewer seizures. I cannot explain that, but it's true.

However, it's not magic. I still have them. I have several every year.

One time, we were at the London Dungeon, a glorified wax museum in London, of all places. It's pretty neat. I love touristy places. Roller coasters, Disney, castles. You name it. If it charges admission, sells hot dogs and has souvenir T-shirts, I am there.

It was early in my days of our dating. We were spending the weekend in London and having a great time. I don't remember any warning or anything leading up to it. I even remember the first part of the tour. Then I remember trying to wake up.

I was at the bottom of a deep black hole. I could hear Sam talking to me. It sounded like she was yelling from somewhere far away. I could hear her but I couldn't say anything. I couldn't do anything. I couldn't move. I was petrified and it seemed to drag on forever.

I wanted to yell out. I wanted to get out of that horrible place. I wanted her to come and help me and I had no idea what to do. I still remember that terrible feeling. It was one of the scariest moments of my life. I was convinced I was dying.

"Mark?" Help me. "Mark. Can you hear me?" Yes. What's happening? I could hear people. I could hear noises. But it was all black and I couldn't move. It was horrible.

Of course, eventually I woke up and everything was fine – as long as you don't count the fact that my girlfriend, now my wife, was freaked out and the people at the London Dungeon were very upset. Once I got up, I only wanted to leave and have nothing to do with them or their Dungeon ever again. They gave us free passes to come back, but when I even think about that place I think about seizures, so I'm never going back.

We talked about it afterwards. I thought, as a doctor, she would be fine with it. She said that she wasn't. She had never seen a seizure. She said I had no pulse. She said it is difficult to watch someone you love lie there, with no pulse, unresponsive. It doesn't matter that you know they have seizures. They still could be dead.

But Sam gives me no flashbacks. She doesn't remind me of seizures that I have had around her. And she is the only person in the world who makes me feel better after I've had one.

But then, I suppose that is love.

Chapter 17 -- Do What You Gotta Do and Move On

That's it. That's all there is. I have no lessons. I have no answers. I have no point.

She is one of the few people I can talk to

I'm happily married. We have two wonderful kids. I still work on cruise ships. And I still have seizures. I have gone almost three years without them – then had several. Then I go a year. And then I have several more. Then I go a month. For a year or two or maybe forever, I am exactly like you. Then, for a couple minutes, I just look really bad. I can't help that. I wish I didn't, but just back off, man. Don't jam anything in my mouth. I'll be fine.

I am in the twenty percent of seizure patients who have "breakthrough" seizures despite medicine's best efforts. What can I say? This used to make me very angry. Now I just deal with them as they come.

For me, there never came a time of "control." There never came a time when I was able to say, "I remember when I used to have seizures." I never get to look back on them and laugh or cry or whatever. I still have them all the time. The only "cure" for me, if that's the right word, was simply to stop trying to find a "cure."

It was all about getting used to it, like being in a hot Jacuzzi. I had to stop waking up on the floor thinking, "Maybe that's my last one" and instead just get up off the damn floor and move on, hoping I wouldn't be down there again for a little while. Just move on with my day. Take solace in the fact that nobody saw me, if that was the case.

Why did I write this book if I don't have any answers? I originally started this project as a film. I wanted to interview as many seizure patients and epileptics as I could, and make a free film to give out to people like me: People who were diagnosed as adults who were having a hard time adjusting. But I could not get the financing.

The worst part was that every person I found who was a seizure patient refused to be interviewed. They would talk to me privately but they did not want to be part of the project. They did not want people to know that they had seizures. There is still a terrible stigma involved with this disease.

Next, I decided to write a book and simply refer to people as "Patient X." Nope. Wasn't good enough. People thought that their friends would still know who they were by the information given in the book and they had no interest in being "outed," not even for the greater good of helping people like themselves.

So I decided to tell my own story. I would stand up and say that I fall down, I piss my pants and I have made horrible decisions when faced with being told that my life was not as I thought it would be. Sure, there is more to it. But this is what I have. I just want people who do not have seizures to read this book and think, "Man. That's not what I thought it was."

It is true I have never really have gotten completely used to it. I still hate seizures. I still get angry about them. I still complain when I have several in a row or two or three in the same week.

But we've all got something. You would be surprised. Cancer, AIDS, MD, MS – there is a list as long as your arm of things ravaging this country. We are just another group moving forward with our lives. The nice thing is that most of the time, we're OK.

And I am certainly getting better about it. I don't get depressed anymore. I don't cry about it. And my wife can make me feel better in an instant.

I'm fine. Everyone I know who has seizures is fine. You get used to it really quickly. It is just that early time when everything seems all messed up that you have to deal with. The quicker you realize that, for lack of a better phrase, you "fall down" every once in a while, the quicker you will move on with your life.

My kids saw their first one the other day. That sucked. They kept saying, "Is this one of your jokes, daddy?" That hurt a lot. More than the seizure I think. But again, what can you do? I got up and moved on. Fifteen minutes later, no one was thinking about it.

I think that's really the secret: Do what you gotta do and move on. So you fell down. No big deal. Just get back up, man. Life is good. At least that has worked for me. And it only took me about twenty years to get here.

ABOUT THE AUTHOR

Mark Hawkins has been a professional comedian since 1991. He has worked comedy clubs across the country as well as cruise ships, colleges and corporate events. He has opened for big-name acts including George Lopez, Phyllis Diller and Jeff Beck. He was the winner of the HBO "Kids In The Hall" Comedy Challenge. Mark lives in the Cayman Islands with his wife and two daughters.

For more information on his comedy or to book him as a speaker go to www.baldhawk.com

Printed in Great Britain
by Amazon

19080409R00054